Before
She left...

Smriti Shrivastava

© **Smriti Shrivastava 2023**

All rights reserved

All rights reserved by author. No part of this publication may be reproduced, stored in a retrieval system or transmitted in any form or by any means, electronic, mechanical, photocopying, recording or otherwise, without the prior permission of the author.

Although every precaution has been taken to verify the accuracy of the information contained herein, the author and publisher assume no responsibility for any errors or omissions. No liability is assumed for damages that may result from the use of information contained within.

First Published in January 2023

ISBN: 978-93-5704-828-6

BLUEROSE PUBLISHERS
www.BlueRoseONE.com
info@bluerosepublishers.com
+91 8882 898 898

Cover Design:
Aman Sharma

Typographic Design:
Namrata Saini

Distributed by: BlueRose, Amazon, Flipkart

Dedicated

To

You

Contents

1. What is a poem?... 1
2. "Waiting for you" 3
3. Minikin 5
4. Whenever it rains 6
5. Dreaming 9
6. Dusks... 10
7. Juda's kiss?.. 11
8. Hit me.. 12
9. The brightest star 14
10. Alone 16
11. Faith 17
12. I am ~ enough 18
13. Resilience 21
14. Experience.. 22
15. Weed 23
16. Her corsage of life.. 24
17. Memories stay 25
18. School days 27
19. Is poetry an art?... 29
20. World 30
21. Wait! White page... 32
22. This isn't love... 34

23. Night o night 35
24. Closed doors 37
25. Girl in the mirror... 39
26. It's easy to die 41
27. I am with you 42
28. Drama of dilemma 43
29. I am Alive! 45
30. Keepsake 47
31. Is she gone? 48
32. I'll come back for you 49

1. What is a poem?

Emotions flooding through pen,
When tears deny to pour off
Endeavour to bring the slightest of change
When the world doesn't bother

Instead of joining hands in plea,
When fingers rush through words
For what lips fear to say
Thoughts rebuff to act cipher

Love, hatred, pain or sufferings,
Adorning as prized gems on heart
Poignant prose weeping blood
In reality's bare choir

When you don't wish to listen
And I've chosen reticence
Yet, you stay there till my last line
Knowing well 'I am not that great Acer'

As your heart beats in sync
With the cadence of my pain
Albeit we are mere acquaintances
You, reading my mind on your paper

It's my endeavour
When the world doesn't bother...

Hey there,

*Thanks for picking up this book midst the myriad titles out there. This is my **first** book and I am so excited to connect with you.*

You know, the most unreal story is the one that life writes on the journal of reality.

Before she left... is a tale of a mother and daughter shared in verses. The story touches the shores of various emotions like love, grief, betrayal, parenting, gushing through the waves of reality and courage.

In the first few poems the mother takes birth and grows along with her little minikin. Blooming is a process, and where wind takes the buds is another.... that's life.

A small jerk & their world is shattered. It takes a while for them to stand up on their feet again. They are fragile but adamant. Going through crumbling circumstances.

Life goes on nevertheless; hope doesn't leave the body before breath. Faith, experience and their zeal leads the way. Dusks & dawns smile at them again. But you know that's not life. It has a thing. To rotate the wheel of time, unravelling the two sides of a coin...love and betrayal, darkness and light, success and failure, and life and death.

Let's read it out in her words. . .

2. "Waiting for you"

Amazing were the days
When your father and I
Cuddled you in our fingers
Smiling at my bump as the mirror gaze

Awesome was the first clue
Of you, coming to us
That I sheepishly got to know
Through those two pink rays

How in the world
Could it be more magical
That we-three have already
Enjoyed dates and ballets

Today or tomorrow
Whenever you wish
We are waiting utter eagerly
With chilled chardonnays

Now and then, my heart jumps to throat
And limbs go numb
The minutes are clumsy and long
Yet, with each pang my joy outweighs

Come soon my baby
Come to mamma and paa
Show us your precious face
N Break this mysterious haze

> *"Now I know why they say giving birth is taking a new birth"* ...

3. Minikin

Tender minikin fingers
Clutching my hand
Rose lips bubbling froth
Nestled twixt blushing cheeks
Oh my! "Mamma", you blow

That blow of breeze
Carries the charm
Mamma holding you
Softly into her arms
You beam at me as I
Cloak you in my own shadow

Gently I kiss
On your bright forehead
A thin line of
Vibrant smile there you draw
I snuggle you tight in embrace
Wiping your wet chin with a poncho

"Time is flying fast...right after my eyes.
And she is growing faster"

4. Whenever it rains

Stroking my shivering palms
I stomped hard in fury
"Why the hell is it raining so hard?"

Gulping down the fuming-hot-coffee
I twitched my brows
At the mud-stained doormat

I had almost dripped off my cup
As my little one cuddled around
And my reverie hit the glass table

She wore me into her soft little arms
Merrily giggling with glee
"Oh, mamma look it's raining"

I smirked at her
Brushing aside my demur
"huh it's raining...I see"

"let's go out mom", she exclaimed
Holding my hand
And twirled callow to impress

Slyly, I winked at the way she moved
And dug my sight into the screen
She was reluctant to give upon me

Just not to let her down
I stood up and we both reached the balcony
Where fresh splashes greeted us

"hurray", she shouted and twisted her feet
To that unsung-unheard-unknown beat
I tried copying her and she jumped with joy

Raindrops slipping through my hair,
Wetting off my shoulders,
Soaked deep into me!

Essence of petrichor, aura of sky
Drizzle of bliss, grey of clouds
All merged into one right after me

We both danced insane, again and again
Till the gold of sun wiped off the rain
Slowly the clouds moved to the wests

We both stood there all wet
She kept crying, "come back"
I hugged her and planted a sweet kiss

For how long hadn't I look up the blue?
Glitter of stars and shine of the moon
Thank you, princess for letting me out

Out of the mundane, I'd created for myself
With myriad chores and

Not a reward to count back
Thank you for letting me sop in wet
For spoiling the floor, a little more
And for making me sip the half-hot coffee again

I'm ready to dance whenever it rains
We both are game
To dance just...insane

Whenever it rains...

5. Dreaming

In the dim light of earthen lamp
His eyes glitter as ember's flare

Lids are sent an invite to embrace
Here, I can't stand his stare

He is resilient to lose sight
As I breath in, 'alas'...he is in the air

Where do I hide my diffidence?
Oh! poor me... caught in his ensnare

As I open again the vermillion of eyes
He seems miles away from here

Or was it the mist of moist love?
To which my frail eyes wanna stay adhered

Where is he?? Was he even there???

"I had heard somewhere that after marriage love evaporates, but didn't ever know,

I would soon be sitting with a glass emptying"

6. Dusks

Dusks are my favourite
Hue of purple and red
Some days orange or blue
The way they bring home a day

They talk to me in many ways
Through poses-prophets or sonnets
Some days they just look at me
Quietly through clouds and lead away

Miraculous it is! how everyday
They make way for both
To date one other
A gorgeous night and a mighty day

The way they stroke my shoulders
Tired from the struggles
And wipe off my sweat drops
Cool breeze calmingly sway

Crests and troughs are perks of voyage
Blessed to those who leave homes back
Smiling wounds are prizes
For those who've survived the day

I had a gripping feeling of, 'when all goes right something's about to be left'

7. Juda's kiss?

Over the moon and stars
Blink! I am sinking into iron's core
Juda's kiss has touched me!
My life sank right at the shore

Entangled to you as grapevine
I have forgotten to rise alone
Oh! How would I gather the drops,
Of sauvignon, all flushed on floor?

Tender petals of my love, hope
And smile scattered at your feet
Now impeach bizarre at me
As if I am a whore!!

"Who is at fault?
We are done so soon love?
Where are the promises from,
Couple-rings we both wore?"

Juda's kiss has touched me
Oh! my life sank right at shore

"I shouldn't have seen it. I shouldn't have touched it...

Why the hell did I pick it up? I am the one GUILTY here. It was his phone. His messages."

8. Hit me...

Hit me
Hit me hard
Once again, sweetheart
So that, I may recover
Your slaps are my pills

To rise from the fever
That your love gave me
To not abandon
But stay within Us
And smile behind the grills

Of cracked trust and vows
Holding with leaden ropes
Now, suffocate me to death
Empty dreams, filled eyes
Who needs one to kill?

Kill me
Do me the favour
But! I am tied to another
I can't betray her
She's so small to learn life skills

To eat, to walk,
To express in talks
Growing basil in oasis

She'll wither if I'm too gone
This thought brings me chills

I would have given up
If it was for me
But I won't let her learn
This trend to plea
She's precious to me as lissom lilies

"In a lifespan we make decisions and sometimes they are hard as hell"

9. The brightest star

At twilight, past a glistening day
He is going back home
Slowly shattering behind
The steep crest of mountains

His scorching blazes
Piercing through the woods
Has softened, yet enough for
The moist to be scared

Now past his swing
From east to the west
Shuffling swiftly
Letting the moon annex

Underneath the dark
Is he taking a nap?
To rise with aurora
Or is he all drained?

The time he was gone
Few posited, "he resigned"
From the arduous courage
He always had shown

But without a sigh
He is back to the sky

To let the days merge
And bring a new dawn

He is the covert ardour
Of every dark night
He is the ace of spades
'The brightest star'

Life is a weird thing... It goes on & on...

10. Alone

Alone I walked through the lane
Holding your breath in chilling winters
Passing beneath the same old palm tree

Alone I caressed your shirt
Embraced your warmth in my arms
Squeezed something in me to set my daze free

Alone I kissed and hugged
Your smell hanging on the corner of my bed
Counted hundreds of stars, till my eyes could see

Alone I waited all night
To open the door for the smile in your eyes
That flutter of your heart, you clutch me

Alone I pulled my hands back
And tore of the string holding us together
Letting you become you again

And me be the Me...

11. Faith

When everything shatters down
And there seems no way out
Close your eyes for a while
And listen to the sound of breath

Breath, that counts each second
Of life, of death
Pendulum swinging between
Smile and wrath

Wrath, seems the end
Of everything around
Pain and grieving lingering
To the pitch bed of death

Death, winning everything
Past-future
The ultimate destiny
Of prayer, healing and faith

Faith, describes humane
The cell we are made of
The musk is right beneath us
needless to be an empath

... just have faith

12. I am~enough

I'll not wait for you
To love me back
To give me hope
To heel me
To feel me

I'll not look up to you
To see me crying and
Offer a shoulder
I am enough
Bold enough

Strong enough
To wipe off
the sorrow of sad
To calm my mad,
Sick little heart

To soothe the torn
And broken soul
I am enough for me
And myself
I don't need help

Cause not you but me
Is the one now I see
I am my strength

I am my breath
I am what I've got

To stand up again
I am hard enough
To stand before me
When a stone is thrown upon
from directions...any

When a fireball strikes
Or the earth quacks beneath
I am there for me
To hold me
To save me

It's my stride
I'll take the strike
Let the nuisance hike
I am bold and bare
To that piercing stare

I am willed to live
And not to die
before I am dead
I'll fight and go on
Oh... Come on

For long I've stood
In your shadow
But for how long
I'll hide in the meadow

I have to come out

With cuts and scars
Near or far
I'll be content
If not today
Then tomorrow

I'll be enough
I set you free
From my supper
I am here for me
And...I am enough

"Rubbing off my moist eyes, haze is gradually washing off. And all I see is what I am left with...and she's enough for me..."

13. Resilience

In your tiny eyes I have seen my dreams
Though you are the writer of your destiny
I am there for you always
Don't lose hope my child...wait

Wait for a while, for your chance
Thrive for the skills to enhance
Aim by the time it all sets
Don't give up, even if it's too late

The clouds will smile in a while
The rays will sheen your moil
Your efforts will change the fate
healing each of your wound till date

Spring will come too soon
if you keep your head to moon
Stand resiliently there my child
Luck will have to open its gate

So, wait my little girl wait!!

14. Experience

When I was a child, I didn't know
What does it mean to grow
How does experience count
Why are the things...like they told?

As I grew...slowly...I wondered
Each day made me ponder
To fathom the bliss and sorrow
As strife of my life unfolded

I giggled, growled, grumbled, and smiled
Many a time wasn't right
How I felt for real inside
But all was worth to behold

Today with years in my pocket
That I earned in bits and pieces
I've seen moments archaic
Hot tempers and warm bodies...turning cold

Parenting is, tough...and single parenting...tougher

15. Weed

Sometimes I wanna be like weeds
The way it stands inconspicuous
Free from expectations. Obligations.
Naive to the ritual of rising high
Green and brown, beautiful. Strong.
Elegant and frail as hell
Soft and all that is needed

Sometimes I don't wanna be looked upon
Rather I wish to hide inside me
Be the weird that mirrors me
Odd. Awkward. Unfiltered.
Free to fly high or low
Game to break or crack within
Off any glitter, shimmer, and bead

And for all that I am
No one shrugs their shoulders
Nag on my imperfections
Or how incompatible I am
But hug me tight
For all that I am
And for all that I am not...

16. Her corsage of life

A blow of wind was enough to shake her up
But it was the storm that kept her standing
A blink of light could ash off her dreams
But in pitch dark she managed kept crawling

When clouds howled at her, she shook, stumbled
Stepped back and forth in the aisle of dubiety
But moments later she had clutched it in her fist
And it swiftly slipped away as a feather of robin

She was in an awe for a while to realise
How could she do that? Made her smile
Who gave her these wings of fire?
All she was made up of was love n desire!

Plucking the flowers down the lane
She now adorned the life bouquet
Be it a smile, a hug, a chirp, or burp
Everything helped her corsage sprawling

17. Memories stay

Images fade away
Moments blur off
People change, but
Memories stay

They do in spite
One erase them
Throw e'm in junk
Or hide in shelves

They wait till
The last layer
of plastic sheds off
from the broken smiles

For the autumn
When arid breeze
Brushes off the dust
To let e'm show up again

When a known face
Crosses the street
Right after your eyes
With an unknown expression

When a tongue-tied name
Rings the strings
Of a long-forgotten
Beautiful song

It happens, yes it does
With all of us
But to shove it under bed
It takes courage

People do change...
...but memories stay

"I saw him today"..."I didn't see him"

18. School days

School days are the best
And so are the school friends
The moments of pleasure
Stays, till the very life ends

The charm, the spark
The fun, the spunk
The games we played
The classes we bunked

Those silly dances in
Shiny dazzling dresses
The claps and applause
Still impress

Assessments and marks
Those green-red remarks
The queues and parades
Tricky lemon races

The quarrels and fights
Over sweet muffin slice
To own a best friend
The other two messes

In a dream I just hugged
Them all once again
The way we had done
In the farewell buses

Buses to far real worlds
Through the bridges of fate
In a pool of acquaintances
But, without real friends

I feel so lucky
To have a cute girly
With whom I can touch again
Those school gates and buses

School days are the best
And so are the school friends

"I have gifted her a diary...
...I have passed on a legacy"

19. Is poetry an art?

Or mere a way for me
To connect with you
Letting you know how I feel
Or to just be with you

When I feel annoyed
Distressed and disgraced
When I feel alone
Longing to be embraced

When ocean of emotion
Keeps pouring off
When I agree to it
While everyone denies

When sun goes down too soon
Without a promise to come back
When ink is my only one
Armour to shine in the black

What would one do?
I wonder and craft
Yet the question remains
Is poetry an art?

20. World

World: a big word
So many worlds
With in each one
Oh! petite world

World of boys and girls
Of caps and curls,
Blue and pink,
Defining their world

Women win there
Men love
Hugs and kisses
What a beautiful world!

& World another
That we don't consider
Words are hideous,
Bare is the world

Where girls are scared and silent
Men beat and prowl them
Keeps mum, she acts slave
Have you heard of that world?

We see young girls all dressed
Ready to chase dreams
While somewhere distant
A well's swallowing her inward

Fathers die for dowry
Daughter burnt alive
How did they get this news?
Where is that world?

Hikes, treats, meets and summits
Matter of one world
Next day's bread is hard to earn
In the huts of the other world!

21. Wait! White page

Wait! White page! Wait!
I know, I surely do,
You wanna get coloured!
Aren't you?

With the crimson of my smile
Or saffron of joy
Emerald of my iris
Or sandal of skin so coy

But all I've got is 'RED' today
Not from the sun
But from my heart
Cracking into pieces with dismay

Still, if you wish
I'll share some grey of my grief
Or splash some sage of sorrow
Onto you today

Else you wait for tomorrow
I'll shed them on my pillow tonight
Drawing a pale rainbow
On the canvas of the naïve night

And I'll come back to you
With a fresh bright smile
Possibly a lighter heart
But let me be tonight

Wait! O crisp white page!
I know you wanna get coloured!

"It's been a while now. She has grown up into a beautiful teenager. I am excited and nervous for her. Now I can no longer keep a tab on her. She has her own life. And I have to let her be...I am scared and happy..."

Next is from her personal diary.

22. This isn't love

Breeze is not lullabying
Beats not skipping
No butterfly dancing in belly
Neither, an amorous air

My cheeks are pink
Dress flaunting a little
Eyes no dreamy for sure
I can see other friends as well

Albeit feels weird
To see him now and then
As soon as he departs
My heart longs for him again

I wanna be with him
While he freezes his stare
I don't blink in between
Gawking in awe at each other

My bestie's sure I do
But I don't have a crush
Nothing in me has changed
This isn't love...

23. Night o night

Night o night
Sit by my side
Dressed in gorgeous black

Night o night
Hug me tight
Let's talk of the eventide

Night o night
How I see you gloomy
Of this solace and alienation

Night o night
Futile are those dreaded
Safe behind concrete walls

Night o night
You've got me with you
When the sea howls to scare you

Night o night
Hold my hand
We'll face it together now on

Night o night
Let the owls growl
It's music to us both

Night o night
Don't be scared
I am with you till dawn

"I know people, who are scared of nights."

"What have they seen?"

24. Closed doors

Black of the blue challenging my fear
Scaring my essence to tremble
As I walked down the lane, stumbled
I was alone and moreover, a girl

I brushed aside the growing worries
Pulling on my socks of courage
I stepped out from the class in the dark
Eerie of silence waiting at bay

Dogs were howling at distance
Tearing off the sky apart
Stones in my feet were testing me
I didn't turn around to have a sight

As I reached the circle for my lane
A hushed sigh of relief escaped
A whistle of familiarity braced me
I was about to reach home now

A meek figure grew closer slowly
The shadow made its way to see
That known face greeted me casually
But something felt surreal to me! Sudden

That brazen fiend hurled to plunder
And clutched the fist I had kept ready

Pepper slipped, dropped down on the road
Alongside I was scattering on the floor

He hovered around me tight and close
A few more hounds were in approach
Prey was caught screeches muffled
Doors kept shut, night began to mourn

This is not the first. she has seen this before
Thousands a time if she least recalls
Dame succumbed under the veil of shame
None such girl has a name

Houses all shut keeping secrets
Until out there is a girl of its own
Until screams start melting the glass off
Or another candle march calls on

I lay there like a stray dog
Eyes surrendered to the night fog
What's left to write or read
There's nothing new...F... melancholy

"Our world has changed... forever"

25. Girl in the mirror

Blurred image of a girl
Stares at me in the mirror
Scars on her face bandaged
Blue lips, puffed lids make me shiver

Eyes dumbstruck and parched
Have lost dreams that night
Deep wounds all over,
Cry hard woes of her

She has lost enough in the plight
Spirit, smile, colours and light
All she's left with a corporeal frame
And I am scared to look at her

She asks unsaid myriads to me
I have nothing in me to reply
She stares at me all blank and aloof
We both are the *Only* for each other

Where is the innocence and naivety?
Which she wore that night onto her
All robbed layer by layer
What is this filth- horror?

Where have I lost myself
In the way of reaching nowhere
We both cry for hours
Hugging onto the fateful mirror

26. It's easy to die

It's easy to die, way easier
Than to live
And moreover
Try to live each passing day

Each minute, each second
Try to breath hard
When inside wants to quit
And you pretend to be alive

It's easy
To shut off eyes
But how to hide from the eyes of this world
Standing up each time and fail miserably

It's tough, it's hard it's enough
And moreover heart-breaking
To face the fake world
As if I'm the culprit no.. no.. *Sinner*

How nice would it have been?
If I could choose to leave
When it's unbearable-unliveable
But all we've got to do is 'not to die'

27. I am with you

When this ambrosial world
Doesn't seem enough
To adore your weary pink eyes
Look beside *sweety*,
Holding your damp palm
I am there with you

When misery cries & howls
Snivels turn into sobs
Bursting down the bridges of calm
Crushing your tender heart in pieces
Beneath the crippled layers of hope
I am there with you

Earth may turn its back onto you
Let people blame you for nothing
Or if you alone agree with them
But when you'll look for me around
Patting you tired back *princess*
I am always there with you

"We have never seen a court from inside.
We have to attend the hearing tomorrow."

28. Drama of dilemma

Poking his round ebony eyes into my soul,
He asked, "What were you doing there?"
His word cut through the thin layer of my grace

I stood hollow for a while
Then a tear rolled down to reply
He was already aware of my breakage

"What was the time? So late?"
Why do you ask me all this?
It was a forced bondage

How did it happen, he asked casually
As if while I am undressing par wall
Everyone's allowed to watch me sneakily

I told less, more I wept and sobbed
Although my dignity had long gone slept
Leaving a few drops of this false hope

That brought me to this wrong move
Not the day when it had happened
But today, among all I got raped

I regret and repent for all that I went through
Why in the world I am alive yet?
What's left for me? I rest my case...

"Words are way sharper than sword"

29. I am Alive!

If breathing in and out is life
I am alive!
If eating, sleeping, walking, is it
I am alright!
But inside, it's all dead
Each of my cell
Screaming to get buried to ashes
Oh! let me feel light
Now I can't think of anything
But that night
How could have I done
To make it right?
How would it had been
If I have not gone
Skipped that one class
Or wouldn't have left alone
How sweet would it have been
If we were same as before
But all I feel now
Is pain and guilt in the core
Dreams have left my eyes
None of the way
Takes me to delight
How long could I be hanging
My body onto me like this?
O God! Bless me to end this plight

I know, it would be sad when I am gone
But I have already stopped to belong
All I've got is this broken cage of soul
Let me leave and take a blissful of flight
All one can see is
I am alive!

Who's at fault?

Did a loser die... or a dead lost the battle?

30. Keepsake

A wrinkled linen
A wet pillow
And a half-torn bread

A bunch of chocolates
Some vibrant nail paints
A nude lip colour

An unfinished letter
Would have been better
If not written

A selfie that sings
Hundreds of mourns
With a smiling face

Her aroma in the room
Daisies once bloomed
Is all she has left for me...

31. Is she gone?

Her giggling smile, like a river
Flowing over sharp edges
Of wild rocks and stones
Hums through my ears

Her shiny eyes with credence
Glittering with discerning solace
Indomitable like a strong shaft
Hold my vision

Her fragrance of jasmine
Vivacious and spunk
Sheer flashes of her sight
Cross my dreams every night

The surge in her voice
With a pinch of titter
Stillness of her breath
Steers the beat of this heart

Albeit she is not here
The way...she was
But in each breath of
My heart she finds life

Justice, sentence, prayer meets and all the sympathy messages...
NOTHING is enough when she is not here.

32. I'll come back for you

Walking down the trail whenever
Fresh roses would caress your feet
And the scent would fill your heart,
I'll come back for you

When sun will go down the hill
Turning the purple into rouge
Giving birth to little sparkly stars,
I'll come back for you

When gleaming children would call
Out your name in stutter
And you would long to see me,
I'll come back for you

How could one dare to write?

What could one?

Fate is the eminent writer...

Destiny is the tremendous story...

Know the Author

Smriti Shrivastava is a writer and poet born and brought up at Gwalior in India. She Possesses a doctorate degree in chemistry and have previously served at organizations like DRDE and FBL, Mumbai. During her tenure in chemical research she identified her true calling for writing. Since then she has been writing blogs and posts regularly on her Facebook page.

Her short story 'Quest' has been published in an anthology named season of suspense and recently her poem 'Love@lastsight' and 'war!' have been published by spirits mania. Both the books are available on amazon & flipkart website.

Apart from writing Smriti has immense interest in music and movies.

Connect with her @

Gmail: *smriti.shrivastava80@gmail.com*

Instagram: *@smriti4040*

Facebook page: *It's all about writing*

www.ingramcontent.com/pod-product-compliance
Lightning Source LLC
LaVergne TN
LVHW061603070526
838199LV00077B/7156